FLOWER

Coloring Book

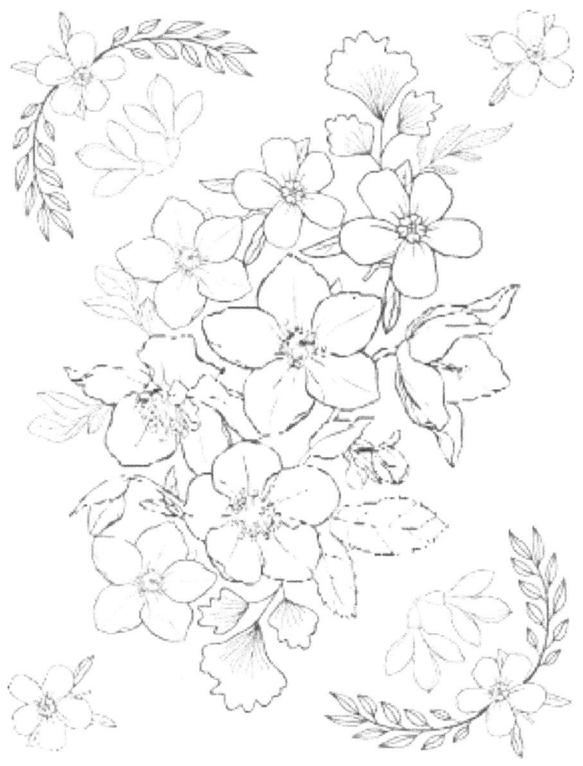

This Book Belongs to:

____

____

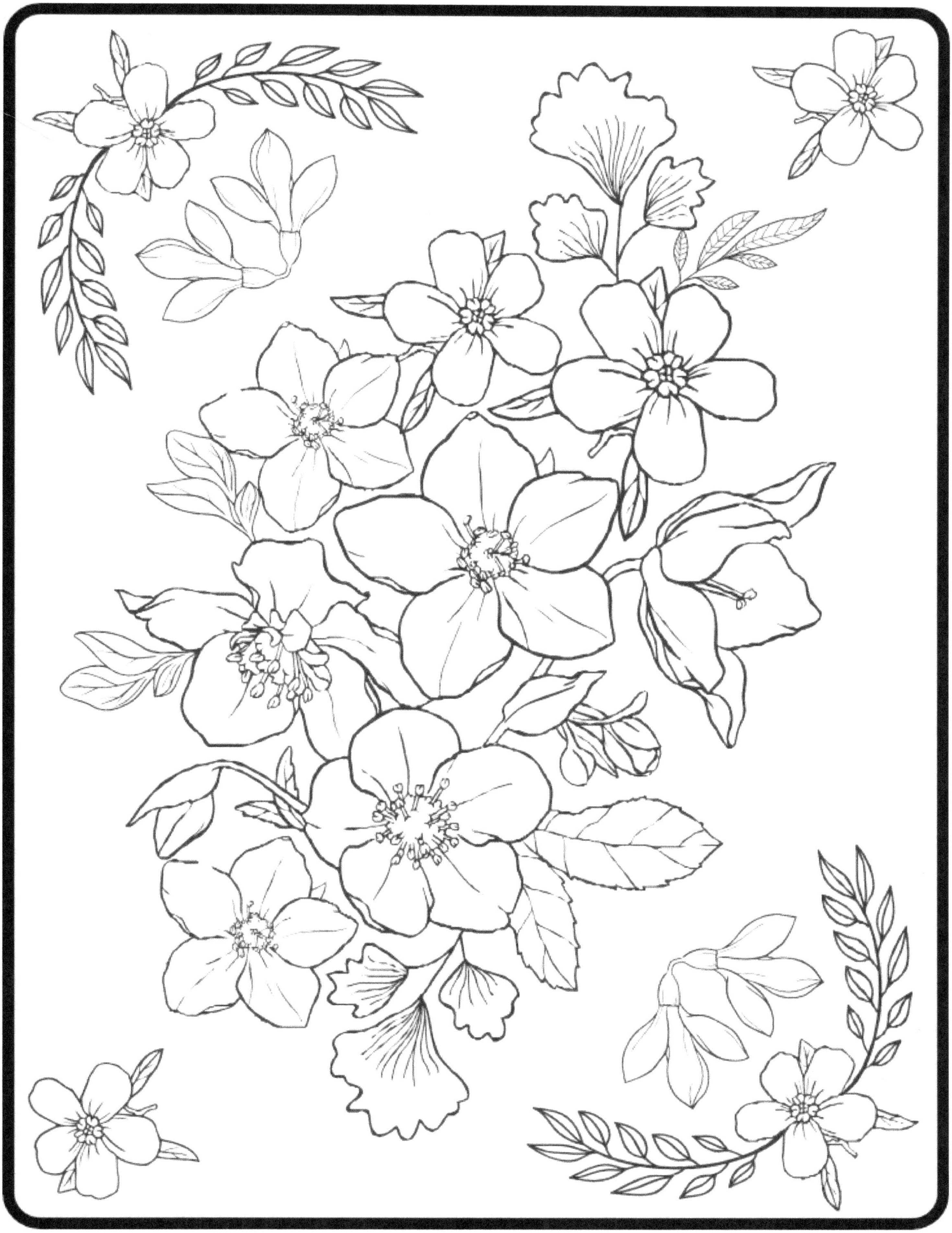

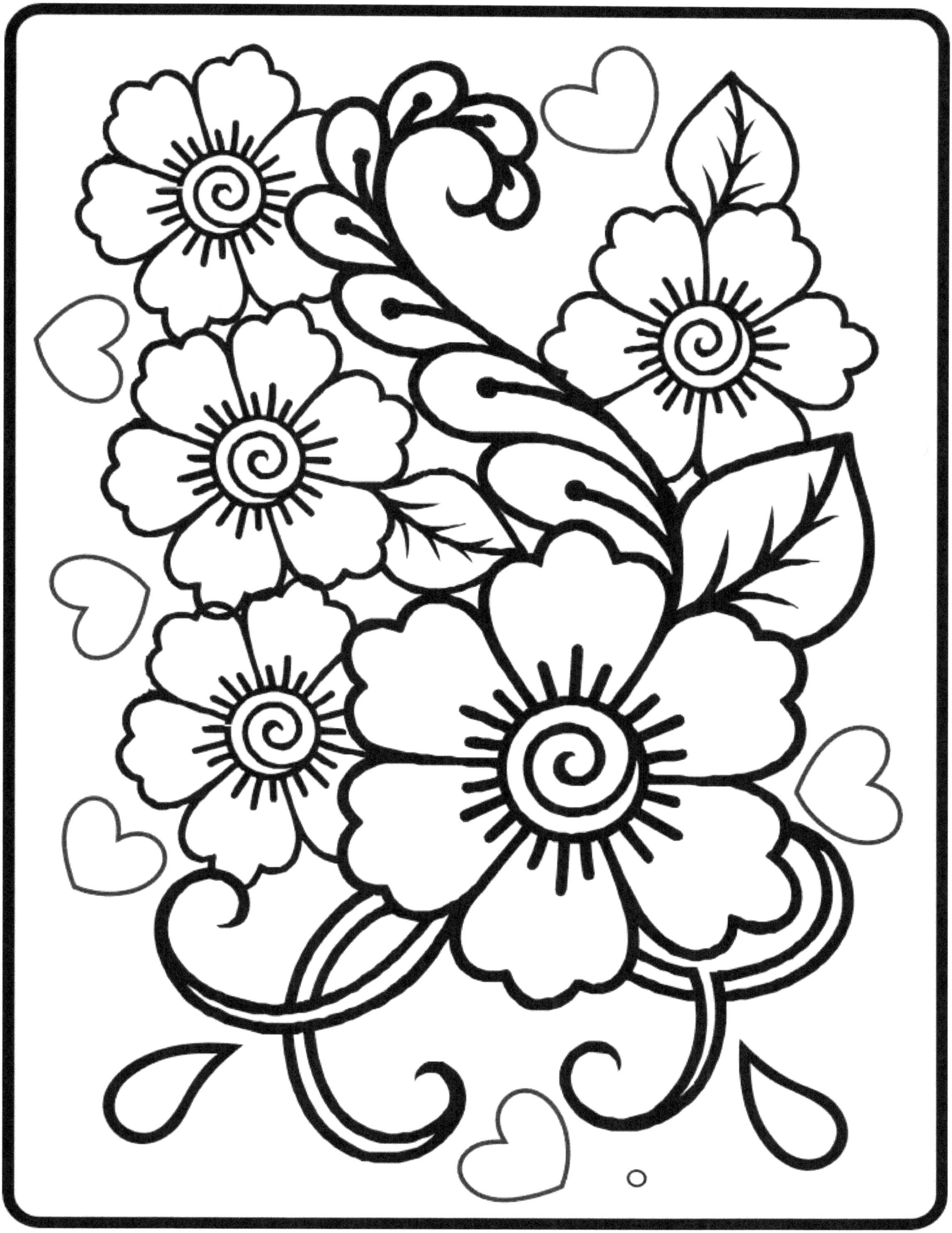

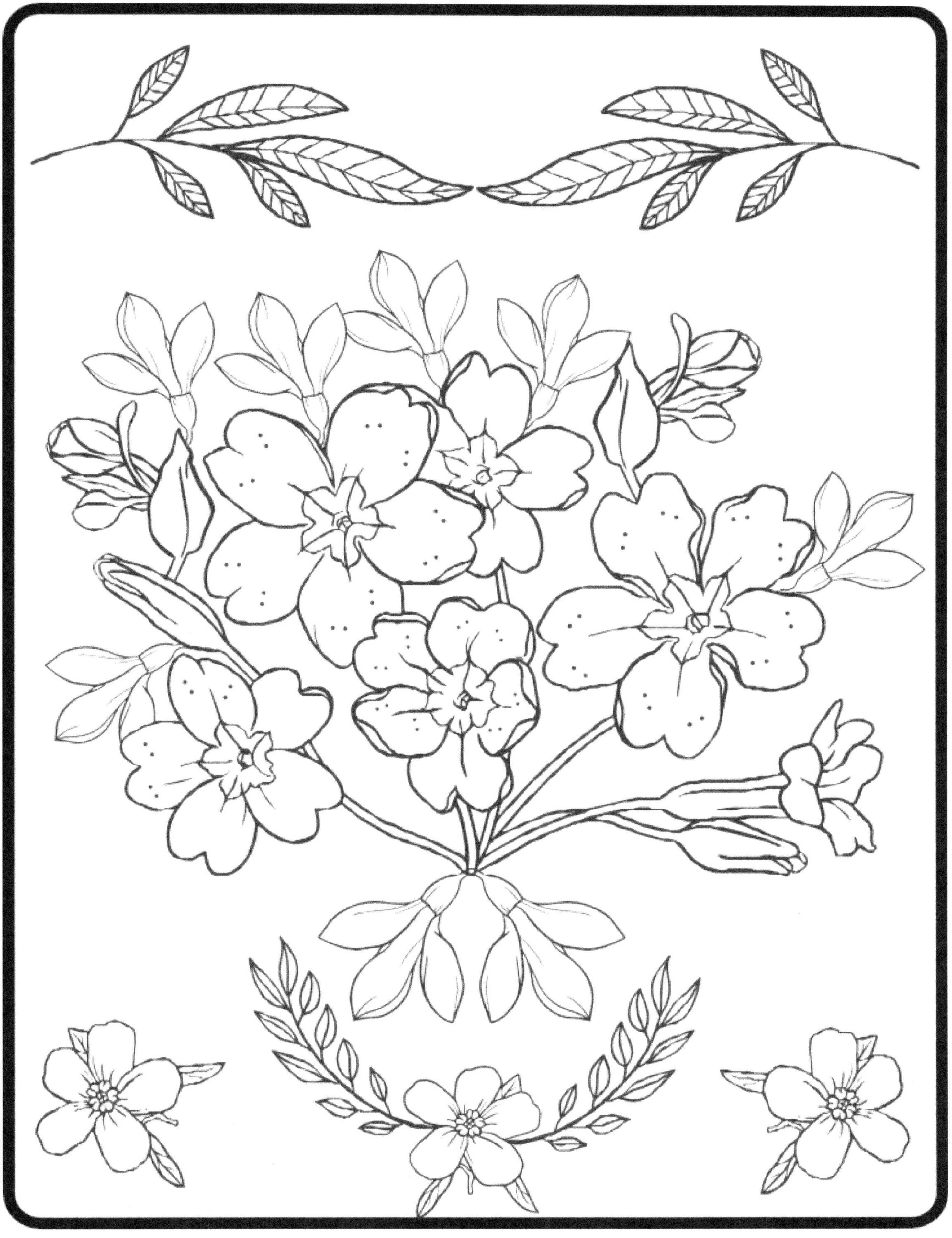

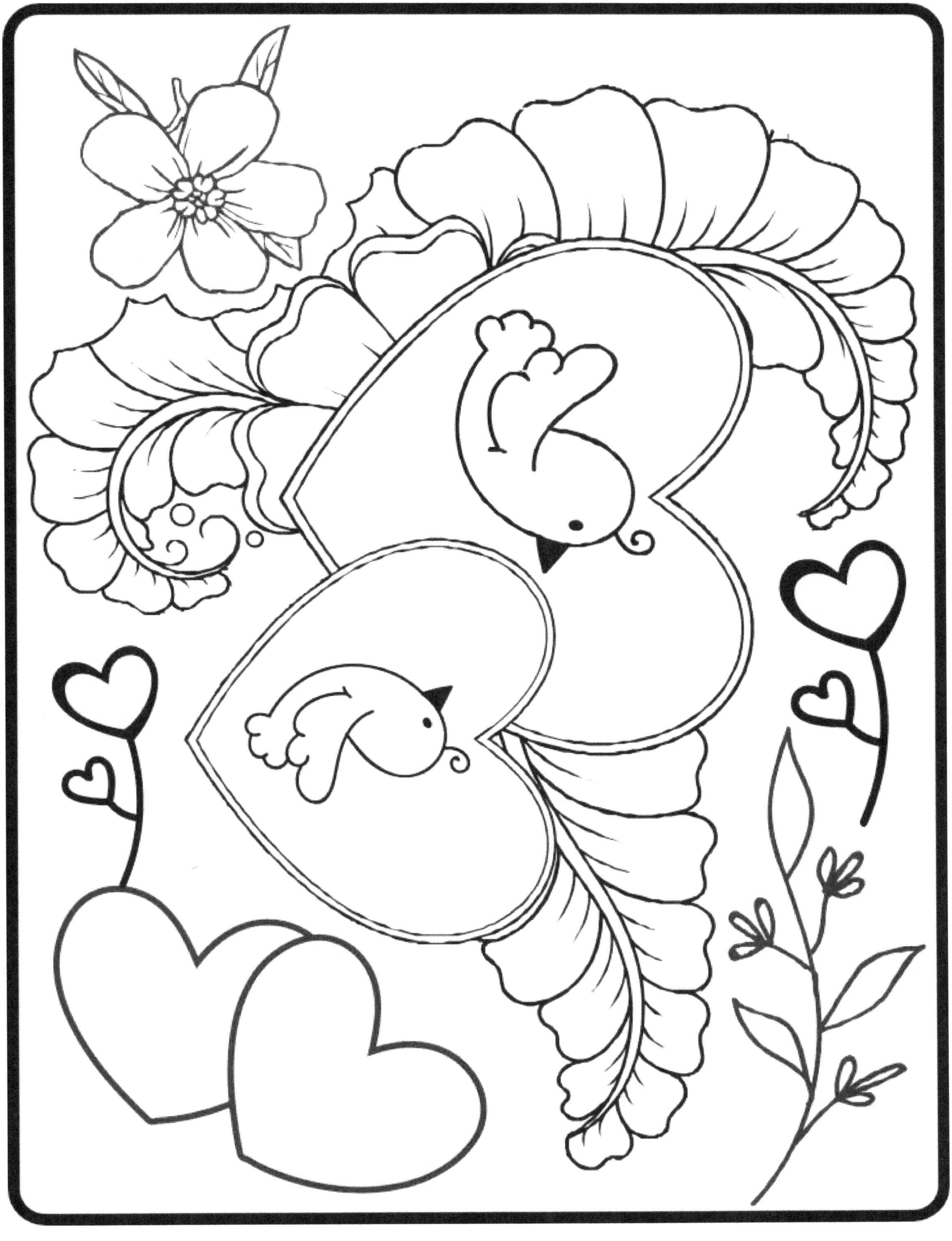

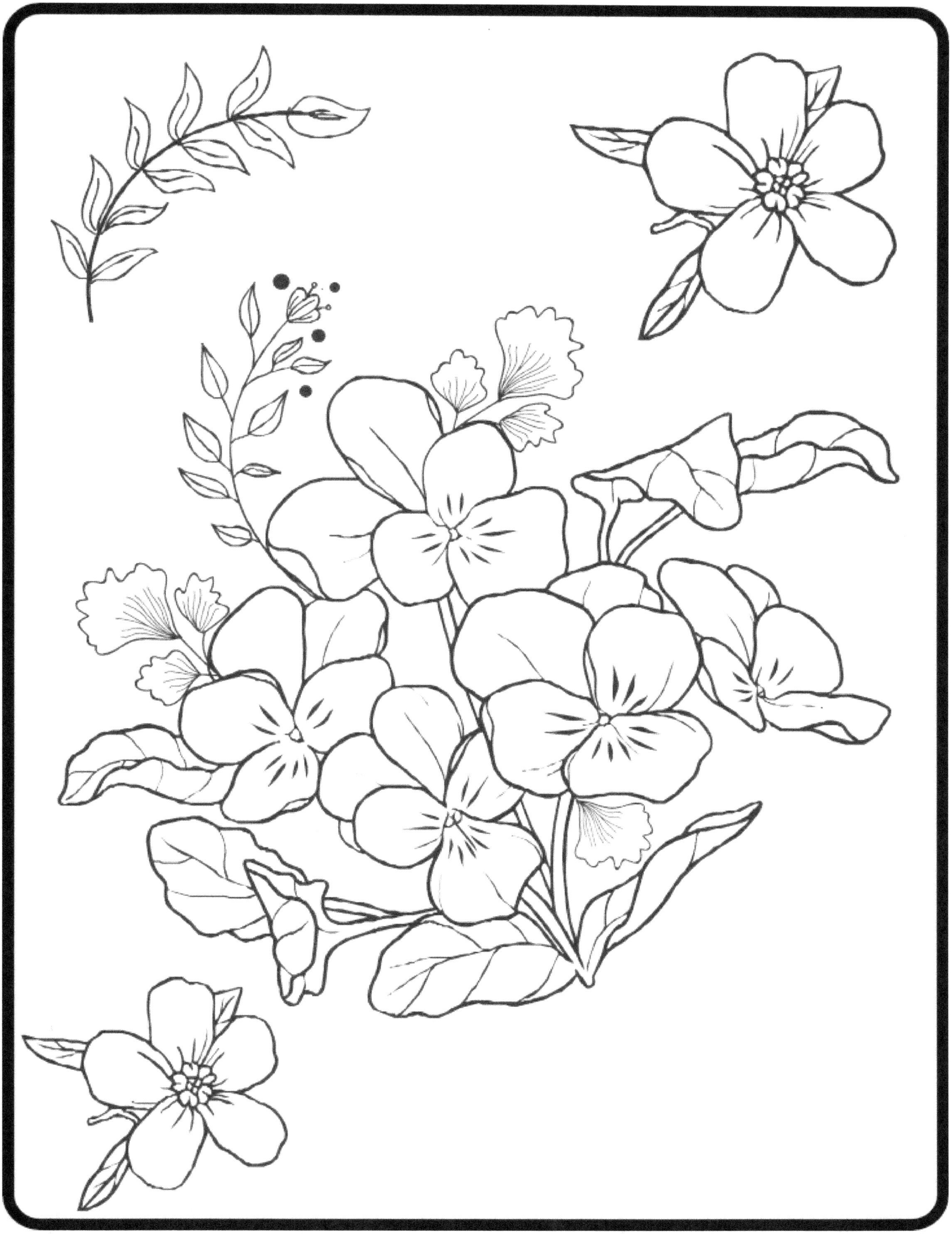

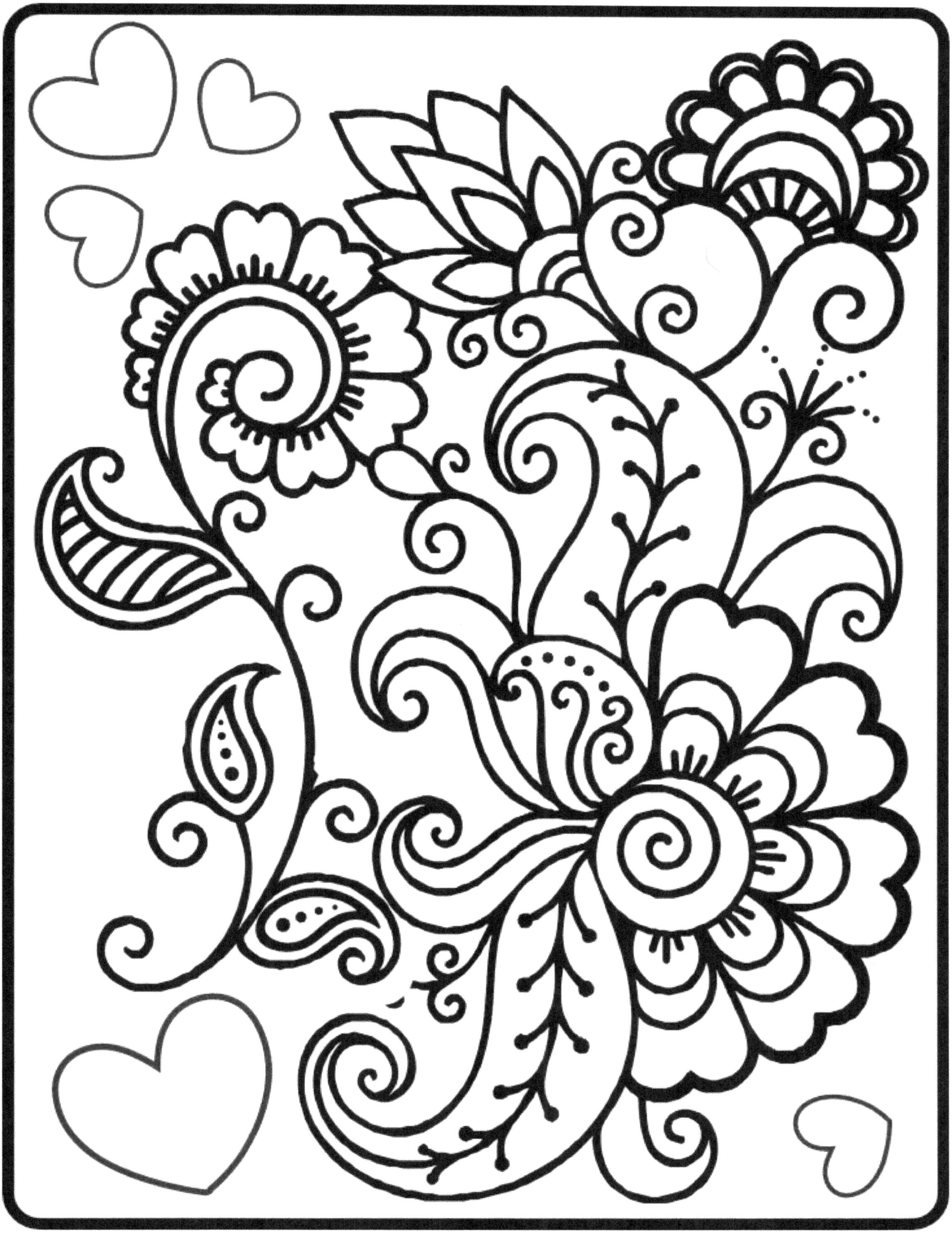

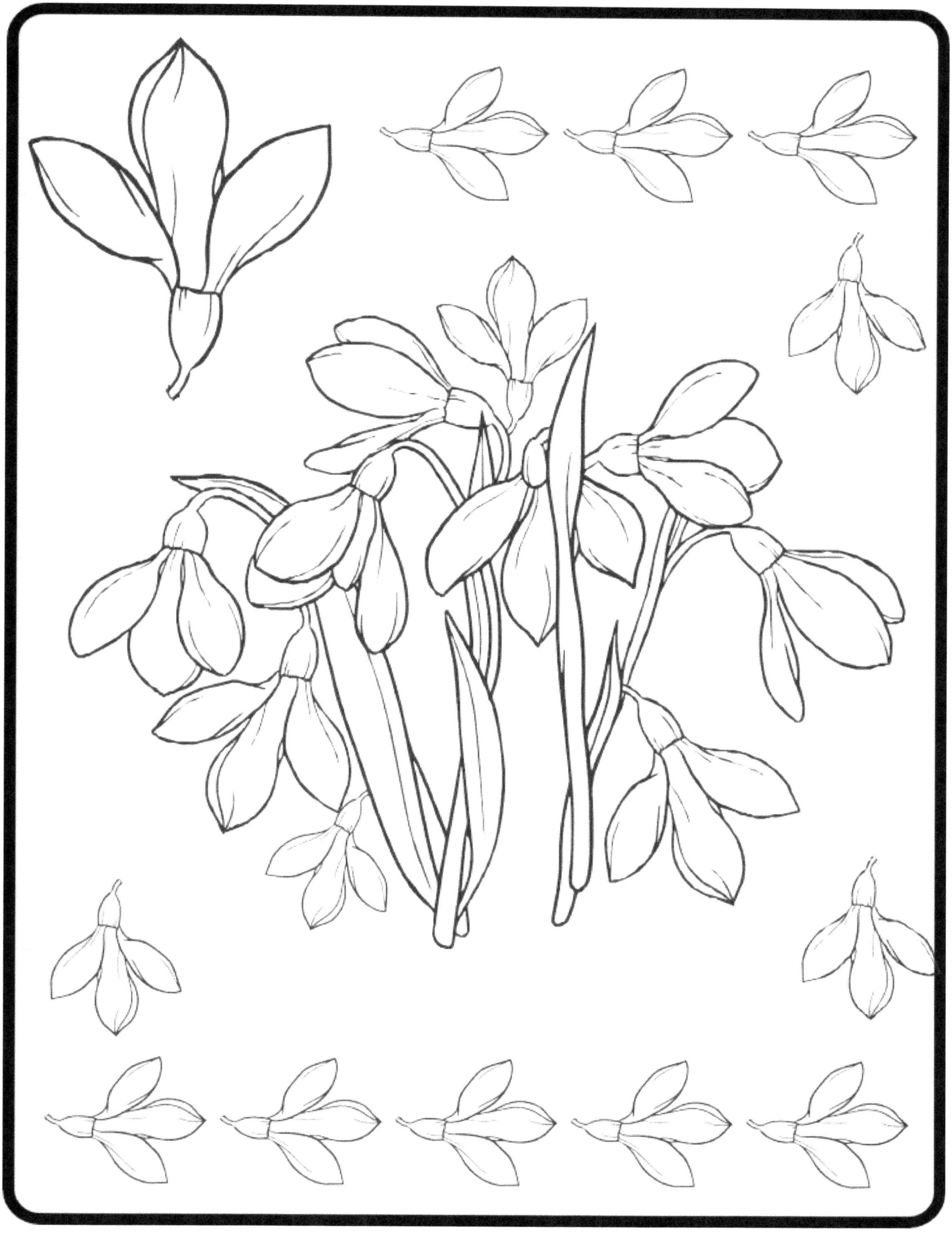

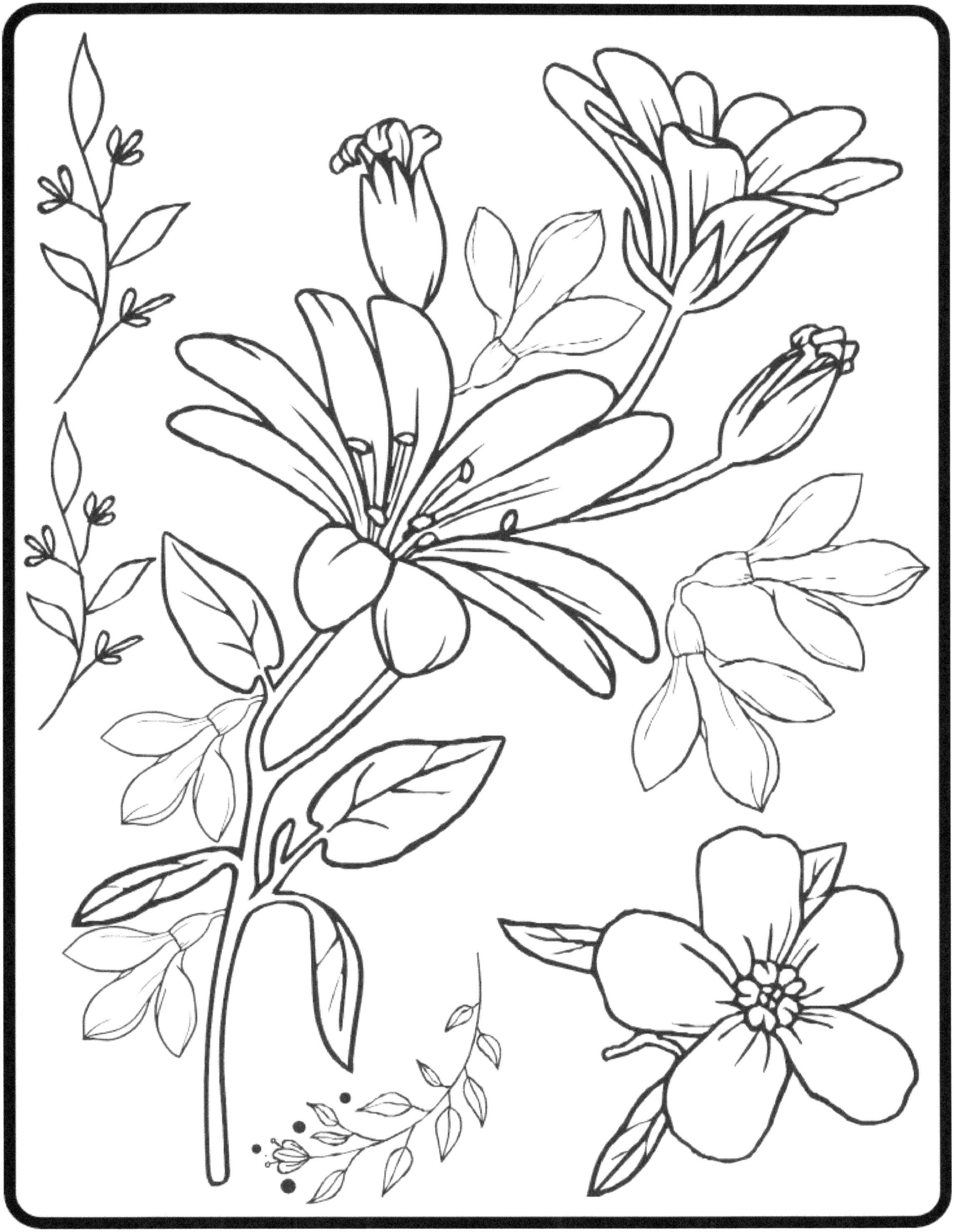

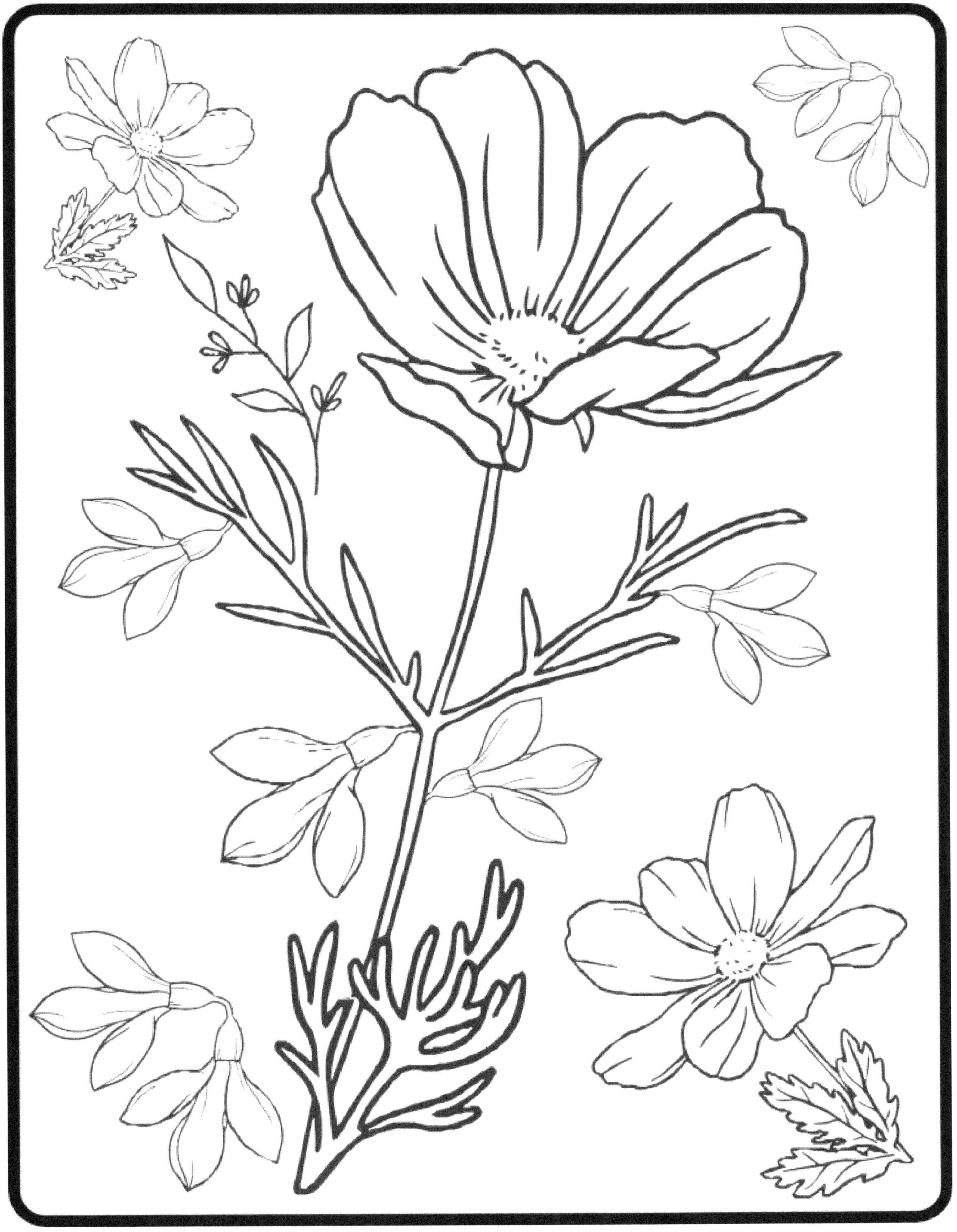

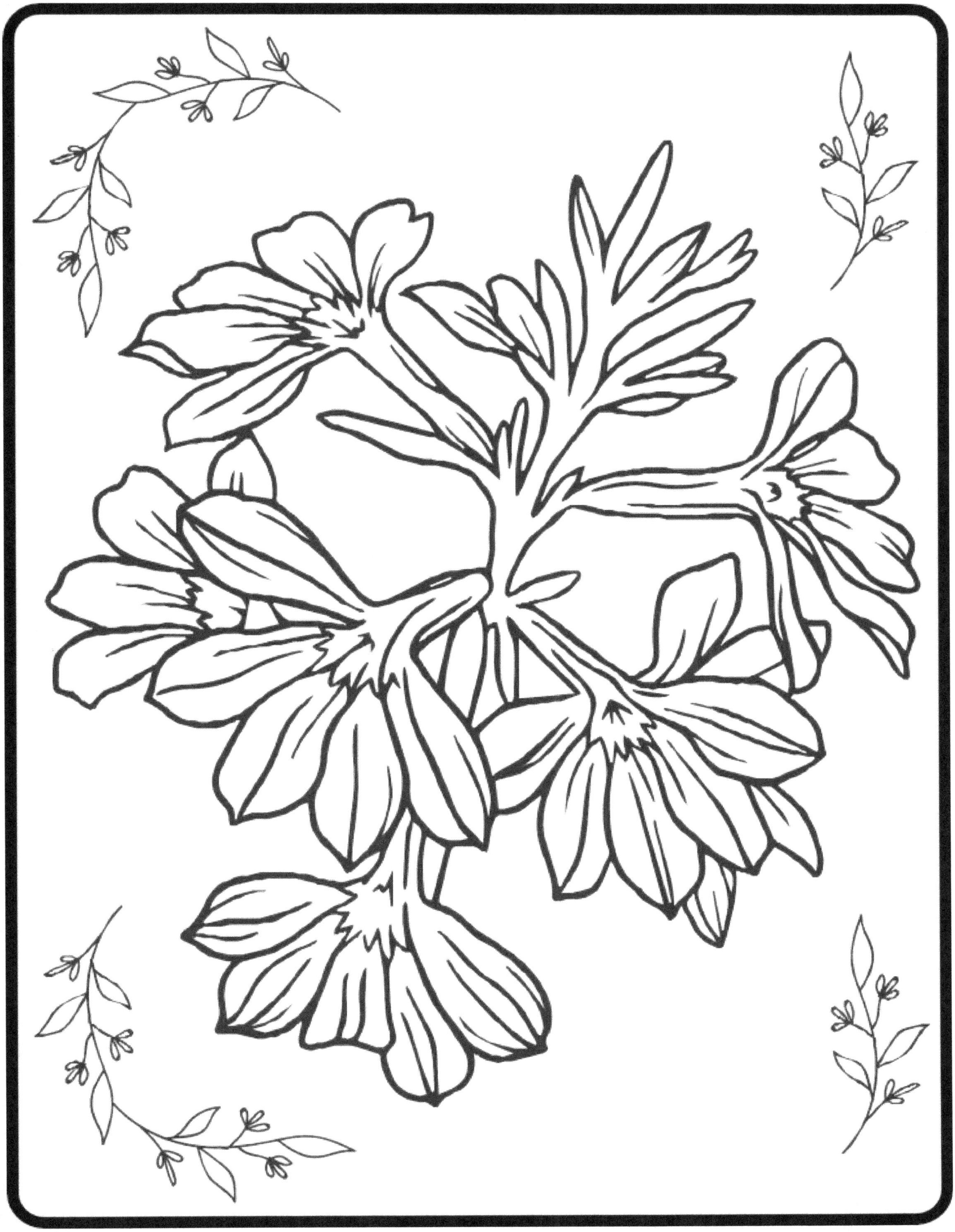

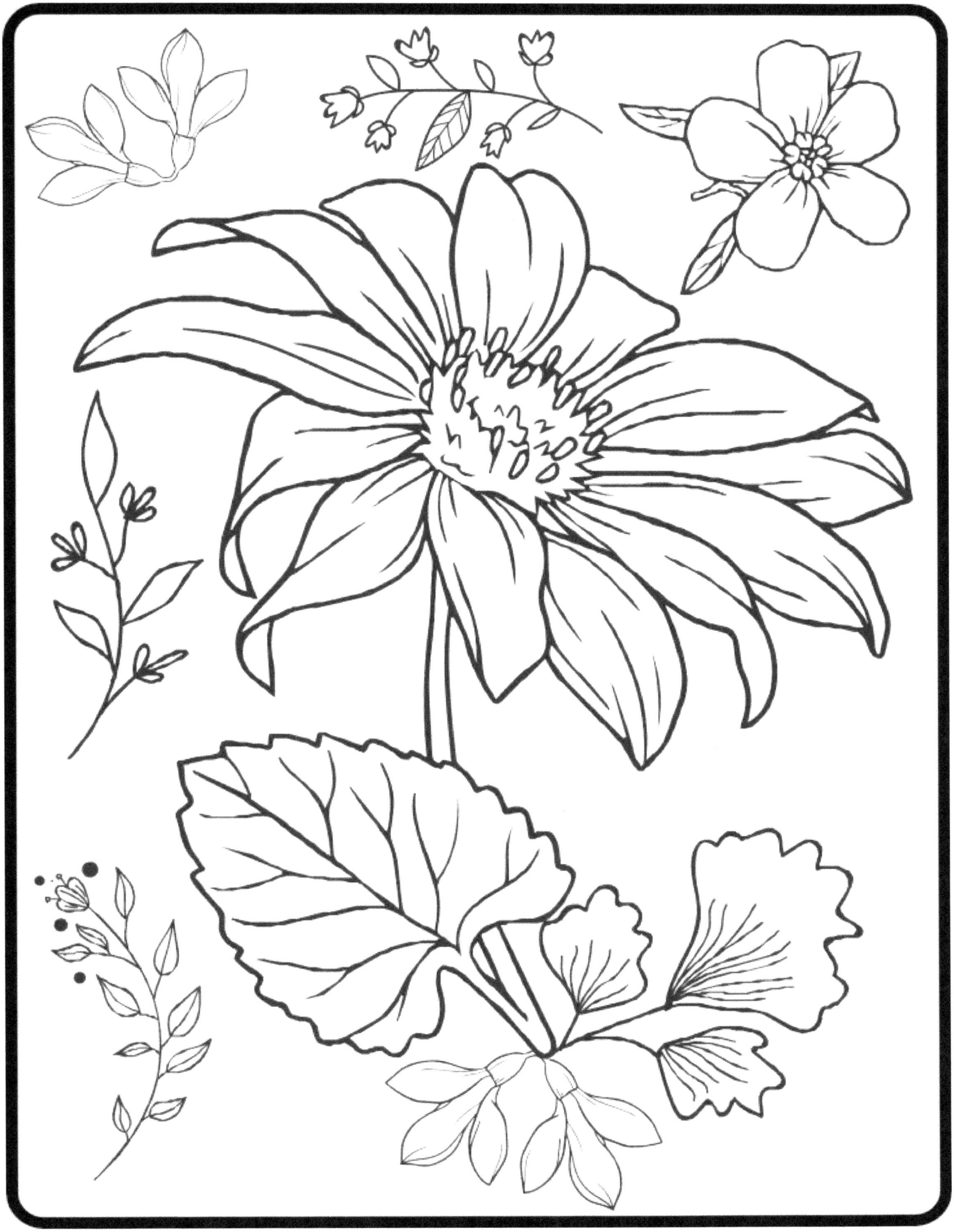

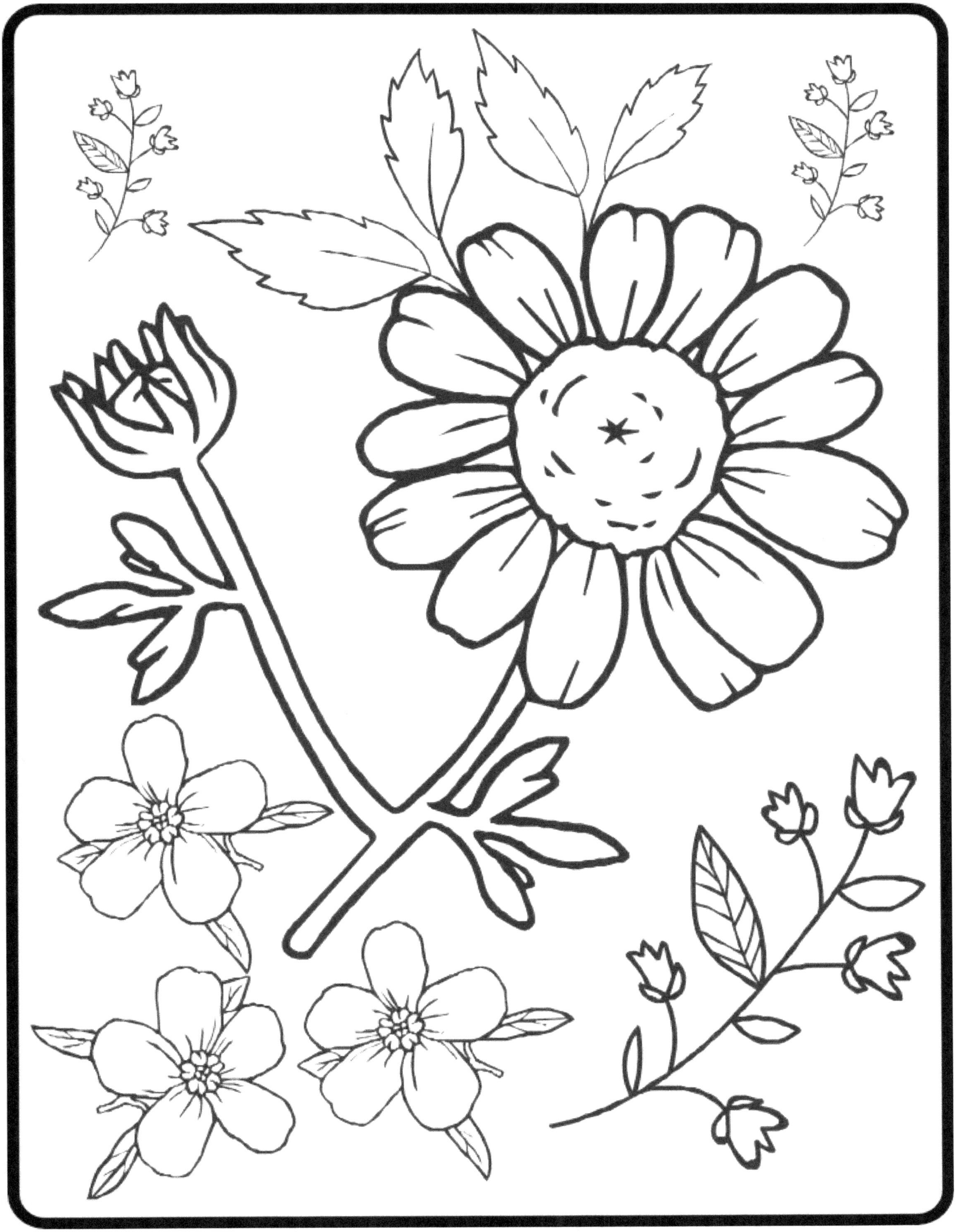

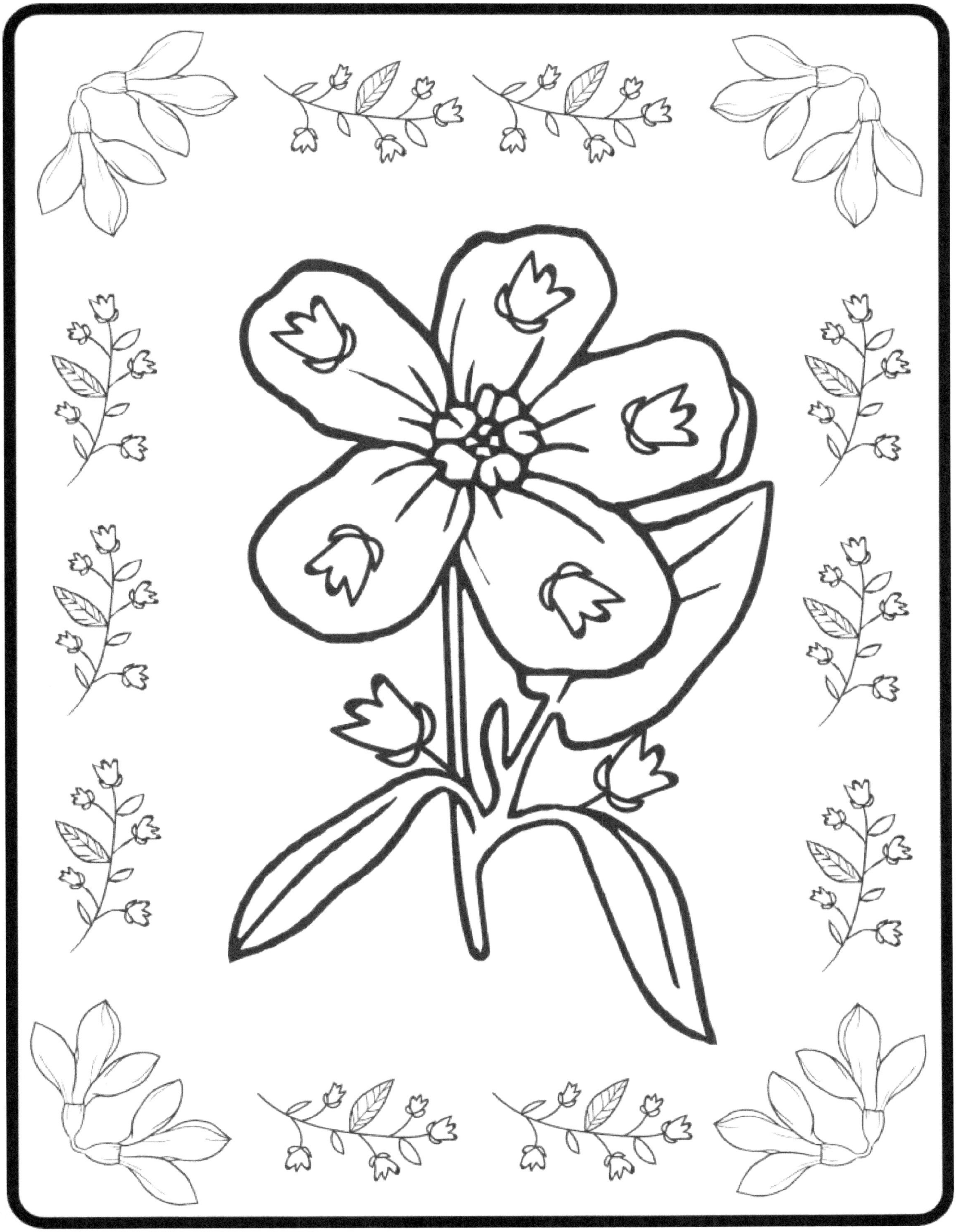

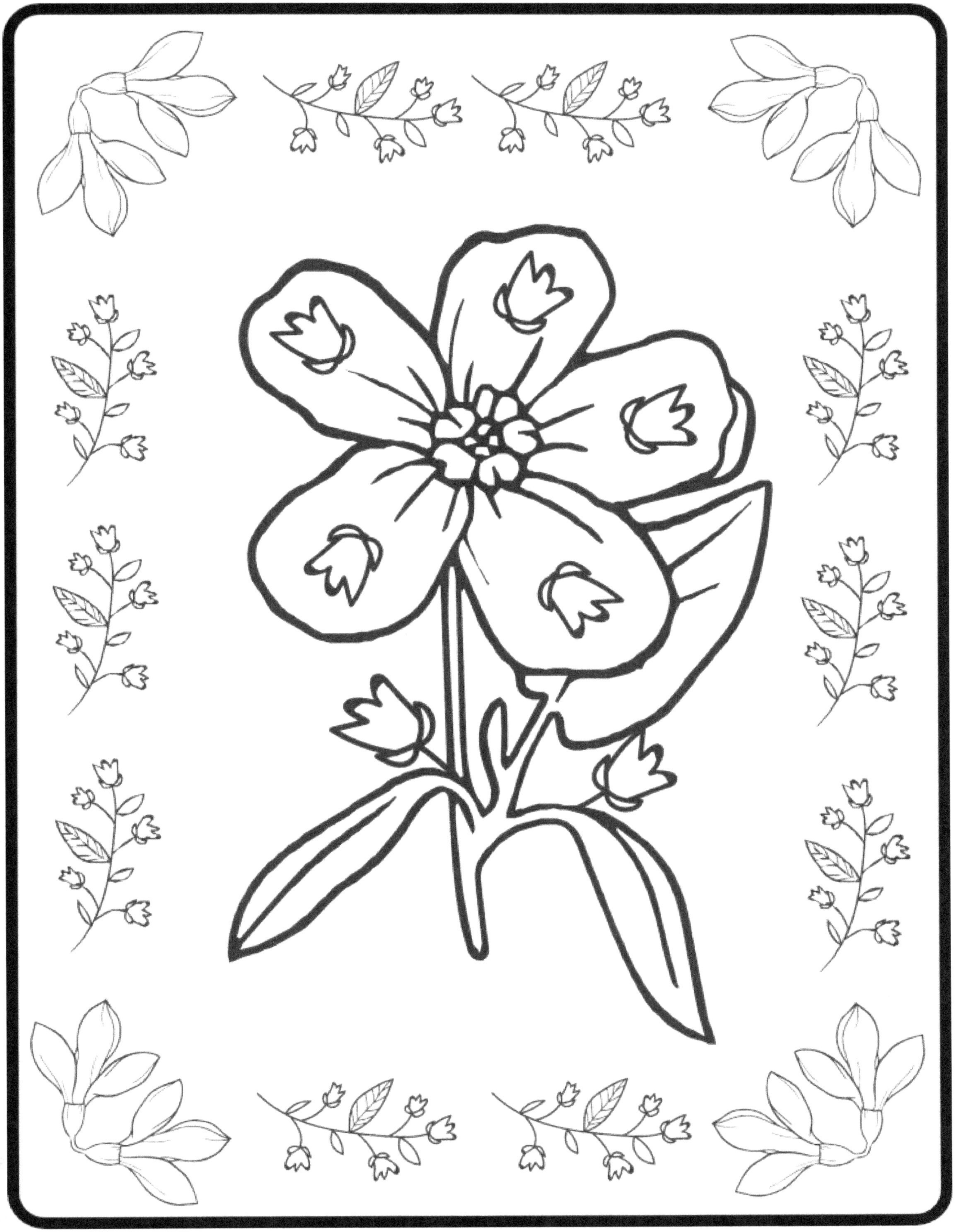

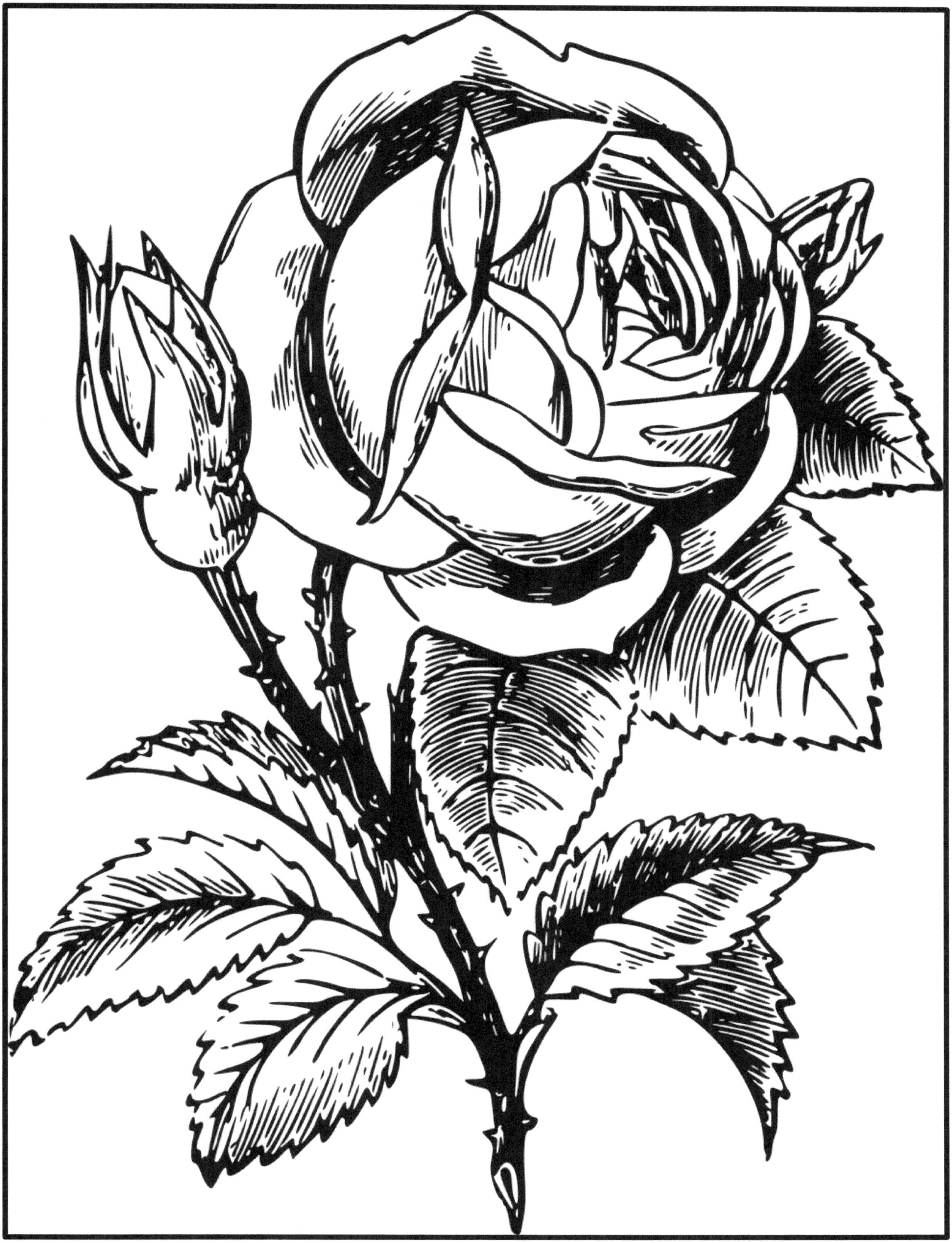

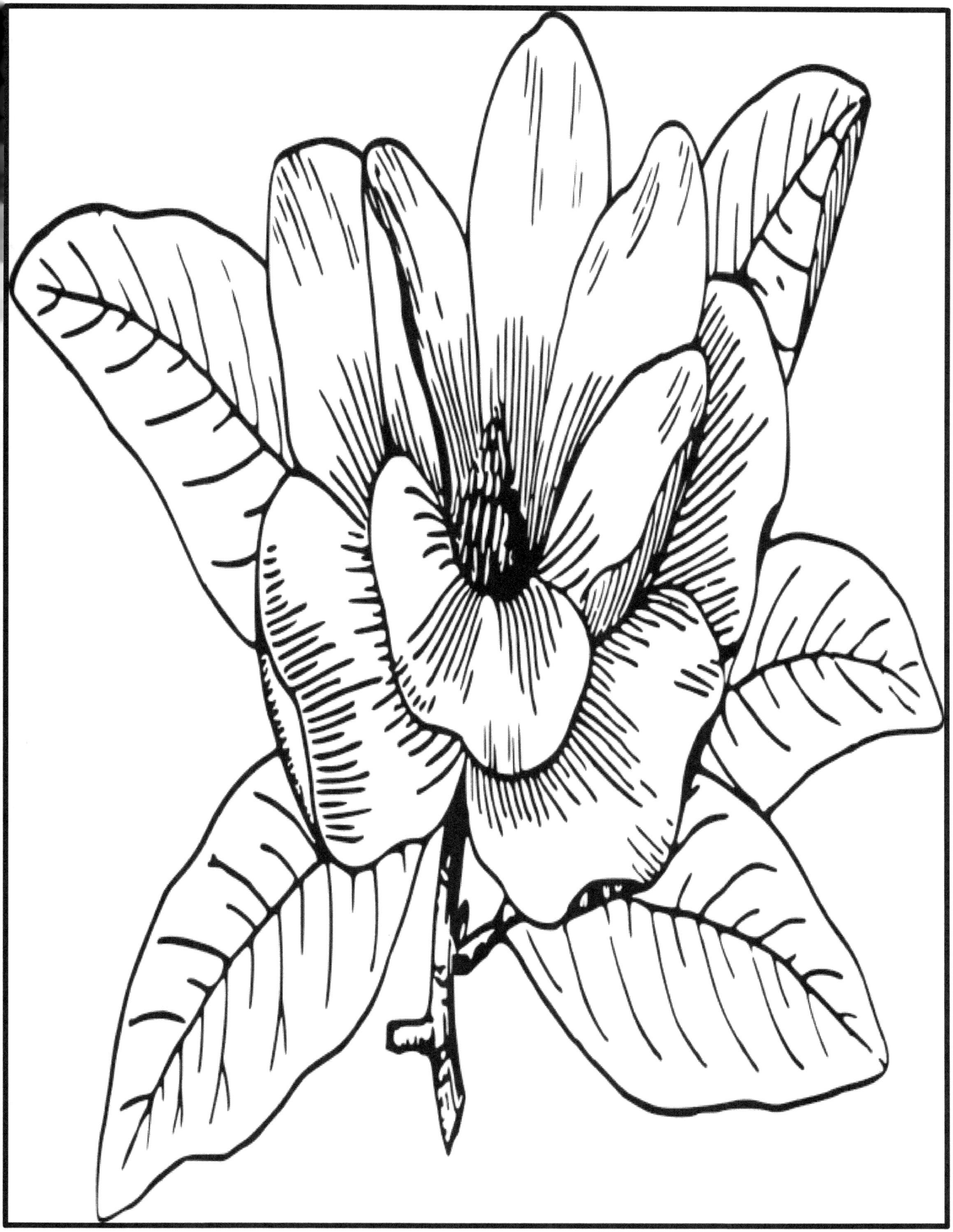

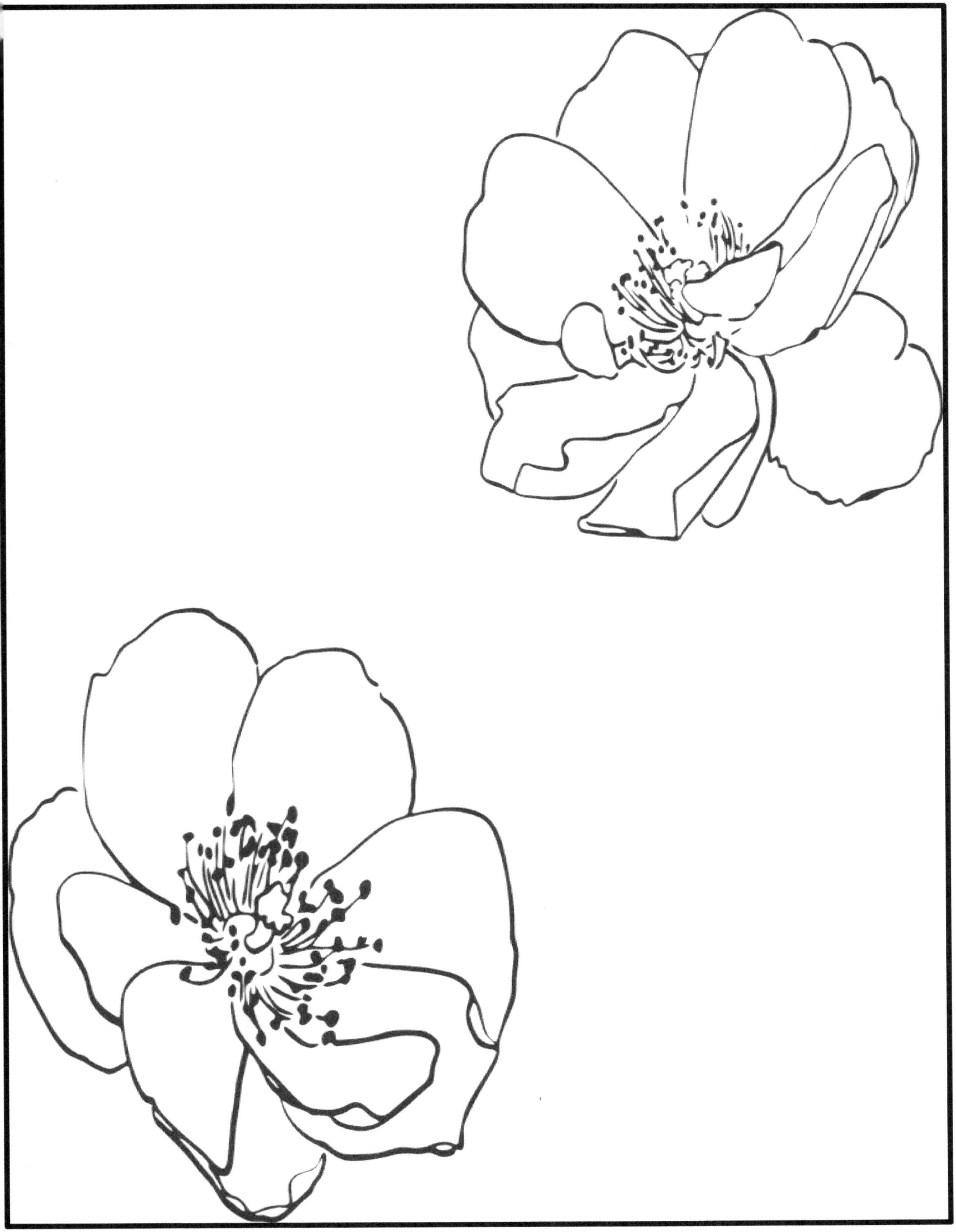

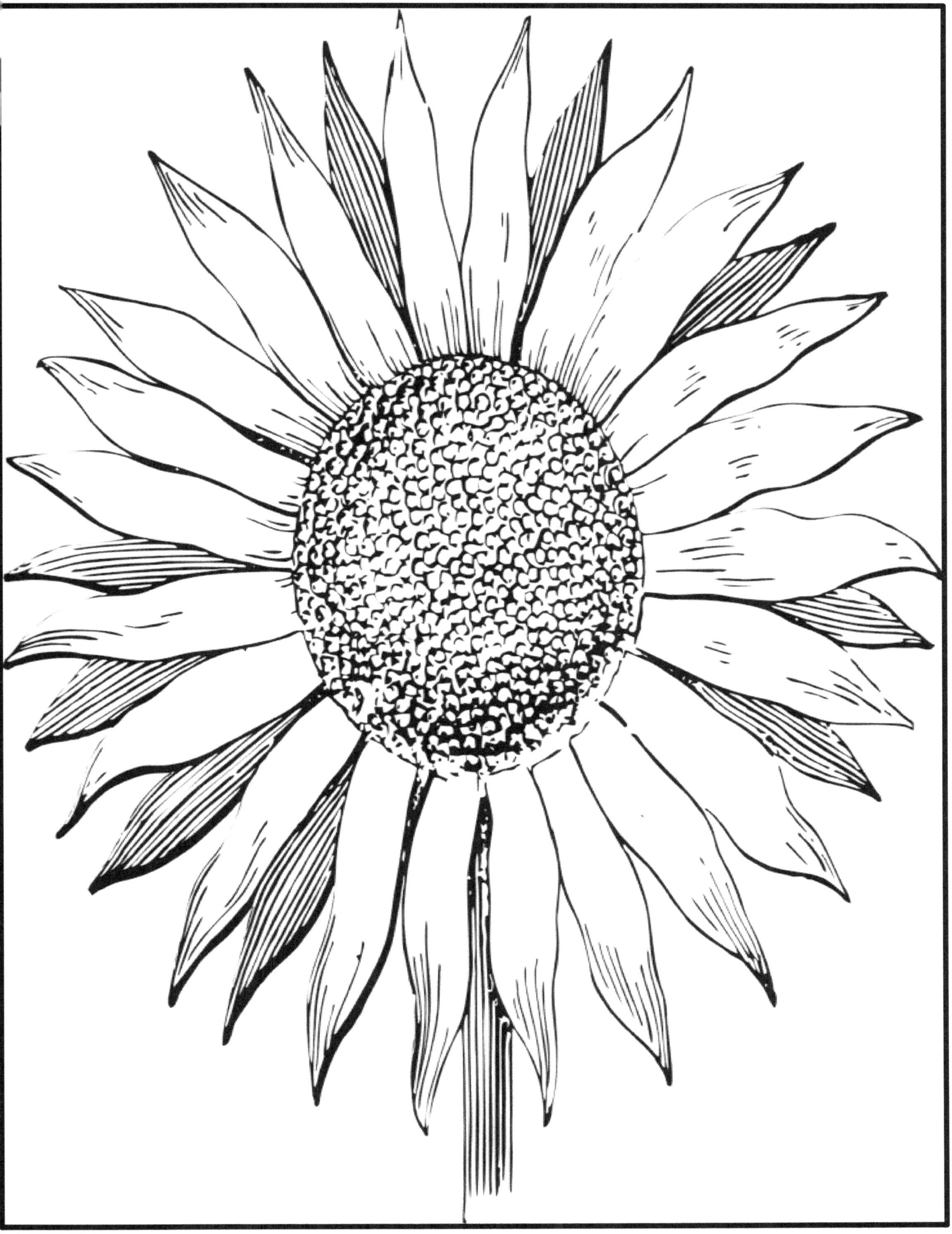

www.ingramcontent.com/pod-product-compliance
Lightning Source LLC
Chambersburg PA
CBHW081542220526
45467CB00010B/3298